TABLE OF CONTENTS

Novel-Ties® are printed on recycled paper.

Copyright © 1995, 2001 by LEARNING LINKS

For the Teacher

This reproducible study guide consists of lessons to use in conjunction with the book *Encyclopedia Brown, Boy Detective.* Written in chapter-by-chapter format, the guide contains a synopsis, pre-reading activities, vocabulary and comprehension exercises, as well as extension activities to be used as follow-up to the novel.

In a homogeneous classroom, whole class instruction with one title is appropriate. In a heterogeneous classroom, reading groups should be formed: each group works on a different novel at its reading level. Depending upon the length of time devoted to reading in the classroom, each novel, with its guide and accompanying lessons, may be completed in three to six weeks.

Begin using NOVEL-TIES for reading development by distributing the novel and a folder to each child. Distribute duplicated pages of the study guide for students to place in their folders. After examining the cover and glancing through the book, students can participate in several pre-reading activities. Vocabulary questions should be considered prior to reading a chapter; all other work should be done after the chapter has been read. Comprehension questions can be answered orally or in writing. The classroom teacher should determine the amount of work to be assigned, always keeping in mind that readers must be nurtured and that the ultimate goal is encouraging students' love of reading.

The benefits of using NOVEL-TIES are numerous. Students read good literature in the original, rather than in abridged or edited form. The good reading habits, formed by practice in focusing on interpretive comprehension and literary techniques, will be transferred to the books students read independently. Passive readers become active, avid readers.

SYNOPSIS

Encyclopedia Brown, Boy Detective, is the first book in Donald Sobol's popular series of mysteries about a clever ten-year-old sleuth. The book is a collection of short stories presented in a game-like format in which young Leroy "Encyclopedia" Brown uses his encyclopedic knowledge and keen powers of observation to solve the mystery in each of ten cases. The solution is not revealed at the end of each case, allowing the reader to figure it out independently. Notes at the end of the book provide the solutions.

In "The Case of Natty Nat," Encyclopedia's dad, the Idaville police chief, is stumped when a local clothing store is supposedly robbed by Natty Nat, a notorious robber whose trademark is a trench coat with a belt in back. While listening to the store owner's account of the robbery, Encyclopedia realizes that the merchant never saw the burglar's back. So, the boy detective concludes that the merchant has fabricated the account of the robbery in order to steal money from his partner.

When Encyclopedia opens his own detective agency in "The Case of the Scattered Cards," a client complains that a tent he found at a local dump and erected two days earlier was taken over by Bugs Meany. Bugs claims that he put up the tent himself that very day. Encyclopedia notes, however, that a deck of cards scattered on the ground under the tent are dry. Since rain had been falling for two days, Encyclopedia concludes that the cards would be damp were Bugs's story true.

In "The Case of the Civil War Sword," a client asks Encyclopedia to find out whether a sword offered for sale by Bugs Meany was really owned by the Confederate general Stonewall Jackson. An inscription on the sword states that it was given to General Jackson by his men in 1861 after his brave stand at the "First Battle of Bull Run." Encyclopedia realizes the sword is a fake since soldiers in 1861 would not have used the word "first." They would not have known that a second Battle of Bull Run would take place the next year.

In "The Case of Merko's Grandson," Encyclopedia tries his wits against girl detective Sally Kimball. She tells a story about a trapeze artist named Merko whose will stipulated that a large inheritance should, in forty years' time, go first to a grandson, and if no grandson were living, to any relative. Sally tells the complicated tale cleverly to avoid mentioning that Merko was a woman. Unlike most readers, who will assume Merko was a man, Encyclopedia correctly identifies which heir should get the inheritance.

In "The Case of the Bank Robber," Encyclopedia sees a robber run from a bank with a bag of money, stumble into a blind beggar, and then run off. Chief Brown catches the robber immediately, but the suspect does not have the stolen money. Encyclopedia visits the hotel of the blind man, and from an open newspaper on the bed, determines he is not really blind. The "blind" man, Encyclopedia proves, was an accomplice who took the money during a staged collision outside the bank.

In "The Case of the Happy Nephew," an eyewitness claims to have seen John Abbot, a local ex-convict running from a bakeshop after a robbery. When the Chief and Encyclopedia pay him a visit, Abbot claims he just returned from a 600-mile car trip. While talking to the Chief, Abbot's baby nephew walks up and down on the hood of Abbot's car barefoot. From this, Encyclopedia realizes that Abbot's alibi is a lie since the car hood would be too hot for the infant had Abbot just driven it so far.

In "The Case of the Diamond Necklace," Mrs. Van Tweedle, a wealthy socialite, plans to auction off a valuable necklace for charity at a large party. Chief Brown is there to stand guard. Miss Stark, a friend of Van Tweedle who is wearing the necklace, suddenly feels ill and goes to her room. Chief Brown, waiting outside her room, soon hears a scream and then two shots. When he bursts into the room, Miss Stark, who had fainted, recovers and says she heard and saw no one. The necklace is gone, and Chief Brown reasons the thief escaped through the window. Encyclopedia accuses Miss Stark of the theft because she would not have screamed before the shots if she hadn't seen or heard anyone.

In "The Case of the Knife in the Watermelon," a boy breaks into Mr. Patch's supermarket and uses a knife to jimmy a window and a cashbox. As the boy escapes from the store, he trips and plunges his knife into a watermelon and leaves it there. When Encyclopedia arrives on the scene, the knife is still in the melon, but Mr. Patch has inadvertently wiped off any fingerprints. The store owner's description of the boy's jacket leads Encyclopedia to the hangout of the Lions, a local gang. There he confronts the gang members, pretending he is about to dust the knife for fingerprints. The boys nervously admit to having similar knives. One boy, to absolve himself, claims his knife has a blade that is longer than the one in the melon. Encyclopedia decides he is the thief since he could have no way of knowing the size of the blade inside the watermelon.

In "The Case of the Missing Roller Skates," Encyclopedia's skates are stolen from the waiting room of his dentist. Reasoning that only a child would steal the skates, Encyclopedia checks with all the doctors in the large medical building to see if any children had just had appointments. There was only one young patient—Billy Haggerty—whom Encyclopedia soon questions. The boy denies taking the skates and claims he does not know Dr. Wilson. From his comments, however, Billy unwittingly reveals that he knows Dr. Wilson is a dentist and a male. From this, Encyclopedia concludes that Billy is lying, and the thief returns the skates.

In "The Case of the Champion Egg Spinner," Eddie Phelan has walked off with many of the neighborhood boys' prize possessions by being able to spin an egg longer than they. Through his keen observation, Encyclopedia determines that Eddie is hardboiling his eggs to make them spin longer. He confronts the champion spinner with this information, and the young cheat agrees to give back the treasures he has won unfairly from the other boys.

PRE-READING ACTIVITIES

1. What nicknames do you and your friends have for each other? What do these nick-names tell about you? Suppose you had a friend whose nickname was "Encyclopedia." Tell what you think he or she might be like.

2. Mysteries come in all shapes and sizes, and they don't always have to do with crimes. Have you or someone you know ever solved a small mystery in your home or community? Tell how using your eyes and ears can help you figure out a solution to a mystery.

3. Name a detective or private eye that you have read about in mysteries or seen in TV shows or movies. What is the detective's name? What are some of the special skills and tools she or he uses to solve cases?

4. One of the "bad guys" in the cases you will read about is named Bugs Meany. He's a bully who is mean to other children. Think of people you know who are bullies or are mean to others. Why do you think they act this way? What is the best way to avoid trouble with them?

5. Read the first few pages of *Encyclopedia Brown, Boy Detective*. You will notice that Encyclopedia's father is the police chief of Idaville. What are some ways that this might help Encyclopedia be a good detective?

6. As you read each case, fill in a Problem/Solution chart, such as the one below. The first problem has been stated. You should supply the solution in the other part of the box. Continue the chart and do each of the other cases in the same manner.

Problem	**Solution**
The Case of Natty Nat *Natty Nat claims that his store was robbed by a man in a trenchcoat, belted in the back.*	
The Case of the Scattered Cards	

THE CASE OF NATTY NAT

Vocabulary: Draw a line from each word on the left to its meaning on the right. Then use the numbered words to fill in the blanks in the sentences below.

1. dingy
2. criminal
3. observation
4. natty
5. mastermind

a. neatly dressed; sporty-looking
b. person who plans an operation, often behind the scenes
c. person who commits an illegal act
d. dirty or dull appearance
e. act of noticing or watching

. . . .

1. After five years without paint, our little cabin looked _____.

2. The photographer focused on my Uncle William, a(n) _____ dresser in his navy blazer with bright brass buttons.

3. After months of careful _____, the police concluded that the gangsters used the vacant store as a hideout.

4. The _____ had broken into the store through a rear window.

5. From inside prison, the convicted felon was the _____ of the plot to rob the bank.

Clues:

As you read "The Case of Natty Nat," write down any clues in the story that might help you solve the case.

The Case of Natty Nat (cont.)

Questions:

1. Why were all the crimes in Idaville solved right away?
2. Why did Chief Brown think that Natty Nat had robbed the store?
3. What detail told Encyclopedia that Mr. Dillon was lying?

Questions for Discussion:

Has listening carefully and watching closely ever helped you solve a problem? Have you ever tried to "train your memory"? Describe your experience.

Literary Device: Simile

A simile is a comparison between two unlike objects using the words "like" or "as." For example:

> Leroy Brown's head was like an encyclopedia.
> He was like a complete library walking around in sneakers.

What is being compared?

_____

What does this comparison tell you about Encyclopedia?

_____

Write a simile in which you compare yourself with some object.

_____

Writing Activity:

Write about a time when you or someone you know mistakenly made an incorrect observation. Describe the consequences of this mistake.

THE CASE OF THE SCATTERED CARDS

Vocabulary: Draw a line from each crime on the left to its description on the right.

1. robbery
2. kidnapping
3. blackmail
4. murder

a. unlawful killing of a human being
b. the taking of property from someone by force
c. carrying off a person by force
d. getting money by threatening to reveal secrets

Write the name of each kind of crime under the appropriate headline that describes it.

1. SENATOR PAYS HUSH MONEY TO KEEP DEALS SECRET

_____

2. GUNMAN KILLS PASSERBY ON STREET

_____

3. CHILD TAKEN FROM PARENTS' HOME

_____

4. THIEVES TAKE $1000 FROM STORE

_____

Clues:

As you read "The Case of the Scattered Cards," write down any clues in the story that might help you solve the case.

The Case of the Scattered Cards (cont.)

Questions:

1. What did Clarence claim about the tent?
2. What did Bugs Meany and the Tigers claim about the same tent?
3. How did the weather playa role in this case?
4. Why were the playing cards scattered on the ground inside the tent a clue for Encyclopedia?

Questions for Discussion:

Have you ever caught someone in a lie? What do you think is the best way to handle such a situation?

Figures of Speech:

Encyclopedia Brown said that he "felt lower than a submarine's bottom" on the day it rained. How did he actually feel?

_____

Complete the following figures of speech:

I felt happier than _____

I felt sillier than _____

I felt gloomier than _____

I felt more nervous than_____

I felt peppier than _____

Art Activity:

Create a poster for yourself advertising a summer job that you could do. Decorate the poster with crayon or magic-marker illustrations.

Writing Activity:

Write about a time when you or someone you know was caught in a lie. Describe the situation and its outcome.

THE CASE OF THE CIVIL WAR SWORD

Vocabulary: The five words in the Word Box are all verbs, or action words. Write each verb next to the question it answers. Then use the verbs to fill in the blanks in the sentences below.

```
                          WORD BOX

     corrected      gasped      grinning      presented      sneered
```

1. _____ Which verb shows surprise?

2. _____ Which verb shows a mistake has been fixed?

3. _____ Which verb shows a gift was given?

4. _____ Which verb shows dislike for someone or something

5. _____ Which verb shows someone is smiling?

. . . .

1. The school _____ me with a medal for winning the spelling bee.

2. "Twelve times four is forty-eight, not thirty-six," Mr. Walsh _____ his son.

3. The entire team was _____ when they realized they had won the relay race.

4. "You look silly in that costume," Sonny _____.

5. As I picked up the old paper bag on the roadside, I _____ with surprise, "This bag is full of money!"

Clues:

As you read "The Case of the Civil War Sword," write down any clues in the story that might help you solve the case.

```
┌─────────────────────────────────────────────────────────────────────┐
│                                                                       │
│                                                                       │
│                                                                       │
│                                                                       │
│                                                                       │
│                                                                       │
│                                                                       │
│                                                                       │
└─────────────────────────────────────────────────────────────────────┘
```

The Case of the Civil War Sword (cont.)

Questions:

1. Why did Peter Clinton come to Encyclopedia Brown's detective agency?
2. What evidence showed that Encyclopedia and Bugs did not like one another?
3. What message was written on the blade of the sword?
4. Why did Encyclopedia tell Peter *not* to trade his bike for the sword?

Question for Discussion:

Why do you think the author had Encyclopedia reading a book called *How to Build a Nuclear Reactor* at the beginning of the case?

Math Connection:

Check the correct box to show whether Peter or Bugs would profit more from each trade. Peter's bicycle is worth $100.00

Work Space

1. The sword is new and cost Bugs $75.00

   ☐ Peter   ☐ Bugs

   profit _____

2. The sword is old, but belonged to a farmer. Bugs bought it at a garage sale for $20.00.

   ☐ Peter   ☐ Bugs

   profit _____

3. The sword really did belong to Stonewall Jackson and is worth 20 bicycles like Peter's.

   ☐ Peter   ☐ Bugs

   profit _____

The Case of the Civil War Sword (cont.)

Social Studies Connection:

Do some research in an encyclopedia to learn about Stonewall Jackson. Find out how he got his name and why he might have once owned a sword. What part did he play in the Battles of Bull Run.

Writing Activities:

1. Imagine you are Peter Clinton and write a journal entry describing the events on the day that Encyclopedia took your case.

2. Make up an original story about Encyclopedia and Bugs. Begin by having Bugs playa mean trick on Encyclopedia. Then tell how the boy detective uses his keen powers of observation to figure out that Bugs was behind the trick.

THE CASE OF MERKO'S GRANDSON

Vocabulary: Write each word from the Word Box on the lines next to its definition.

```
                        WORD BOX
    challenged        inheritance          snarled
    champions         referee              triumph
```

1. called to a game or contest __ __ __ Ⓞ __ __ __ __ __ __

2. winners of a contest __ __ __ __ __ Ⓞ __ __ __

3. spoke harshly in an angry way Ⓞ __ __ __ __ __ __

4. great success Ⓞ __ __ __ __ __ __

5. judge in a contest or game __ Ⓞ __ __ __ __ __

6. money or goods received from parents or ancestors __ Ⓞ __ __ __ __ __ __ __ __ __

Write the message in the circled letters: __ __ __ __ __

This word tells what Encyclopedia Brown must do to solve his next case.

Clues:

As you read "The Case of Merko's Grandson," write down any clues in the story that might help you solve the case.

The Case of Merko's Grandson (cont.)

Questions:

1. Why did Bugs Meany and his Tigers rally behind Encyclopedia in a battle of brains?

2. Why did Sally want to challenge Encyclopedia Brown?

3. What kind of contest did the kids set up between Sally and Encyclopedia?

4. Who was the Great Merko, and what did Merko's will say?

5. Why do you think the kids were surprised when Encyclopedia said the money should go to Fred Gibson?

Questions for Discussion:

1. What do you think Encyclopedia meant when he remarked to Sally that she told the story "very cleverly"?

2. In what ways do boys and girls compete with each other in your school or neighborhood? Is this competition healthy?

Figures of Speech:

What do you imagine when Bugs was described as wearing "the sick smile of a boy who had taken one ride too many on a roller coaster"?

_____

Complete the following figures of speech:

1. My baby sister wore the sweet smile of _____

2. My grandfather wore the surprised look of _____

3. I wore the frightened stare of _____

Writing Activity:

Turn "The Case of Merko's Grandson" into a script for story theater. Add dialogue to the scenes when Sally assaulted Bugs and when Sally challenged Encyclopedia. Choose readers for the parts of Encyclopedia, Sally, Peter, Bugs, and the girls on the softball team. Choose another classmate to read the narration. You may use hats as simple props to denote character.

THE CASE OF THE BANK ROBBER

Vocabulary: Draw a line from each word on the left to its definition on the right. Then use the numbered words to fill in the blanks in the sentences below.

1. features
2. recognize
3. beggar
4. resisted
5. distinguishing

a. acted against; opposed
b. parts of the face
c. poor person who asks for charity
d. identify
e. characteristic

. . . .

1. We offered some money to the _____ as he held out a cup in our direction.

2. The burglar _____ arrest by fighting off the police officers and running into the woods.

3. Since Dad was wearing a mask and costume, no one was able to _____ him.

4. Beady eyes and a small, pointed nose were the _____ of his face that I remember best.

5. A tattoo of a dinosaur on his arm was one of the _____ marks by which the police found him.

Clues:

As you read "The Case of the Bank Robber," write down any clues in the story that might help you solve the case.

The Case of the Bank Robber (cont.)

Questions:

1. What crime did Encyclopedia and Sally notice on their bus trip downtown?

2. What happened as the robber left the bank and started to race down the street?

3. Why couldn't the police be sure the man they caught was the bank robber?

4. Why did Encyclopedia go downtown to talk to Blind Tom?

5. Why did Encyclopedia decide not to talk with the blind man after all?

Questions for Discussion:

1. Why do you think Encyclopedia took on Sally Kimball as a partner in his detective agency? Do you think this was a smart decision?

2. Do you think it was wise for Encyclopedia and Sally to go down to the hotel alone to investigate the case?

Math Connection:

Encyclopedia Brown has earned $3.50 from his detective agency. As you know, he charges $.25 a case. How many cases has he solved?

Social Studies Connection:

Chief Brown lacks evidence and has no witnesses who can identify the robber. Therefore, he can't hold his suspect in jail. Find out what the term habeas corpus means and how it protects people from being held for crimes. Also list some other rights that people have when they are arrested by the police.

Writing Activity:

Pretend you are a reporter for the *Idaville Daily News*. Write a headline and a story about how Encyclopedia Brown and Sally Kimball cracked the bank robbery case.

THE CASE OF THE HAPPY NEPHEW

Vocabulary: Use the words in the Word Box to fill in the puzzles. Then use the same words to complete the paragraph below.

WORD BOX			
alibi	arrest	eyewitness	proof

1. enough evidence to show something is true

2. take and hold a person in jail

3. excuse that shows why a person could not have committed a crime

4. someone who sees a crime occur

A(n) _____ [1] at the scene of a crime says you did it! The police want to question you, and they might even _____ [2] you. Fortunately, you have a good _____.[3] You can show that you were somewhere else at the time. They will need more _____ [4] before they can charge you.

Clues:

As you read "The Case of the Happy Nephew," write down any clues in the story that might help you solve the case.

The Case of the Happy Nephew (cont.)

Questions:

1. What was the crime in this case?

2. What did the eyewitness claim to have seen at the bake shop?

3. What was John Abbot's alibi?

4. Why didn't Encyclopedia Brown believe Abbot's alibi?

Questions for Discussion:

1. Do you think that Encyclopedia's observations at John Abbot's house would stand up in court? What other evidence would the town need to convict Abbot of the crime?

2. How might this case have changed if John Abbot had not been babysitting for his nephew?

Math Connection:

John Abbot claimed he drove 600 miles in just under 12 hours. Suppose the speed limit was 55 mph and he stopped for about 30 minutes to get gas and eat. Was John Abbot telling the truth when he said he did not break any speed limits?

Science Connection:

Use a thermometer to measure the temperature of the hood of a car after it has been running for an hour. Would this temperature be too hot to walk on comfortably? Heat from burning gasoline would melt a car's metal engine parts were it not for the cooling system. Find a diagram that shows how water or antifreeze is cooled in a car radiator and then sent through the water jacket to cool the cylinders.

Writing Activity:

Pretend you are Chief Brown. Write a police report that tells about your meeting with John Abbot. Tell everything that happened. Then indicate what you think you could do to check Abbot's alibi.

THE CASE OF THE DIAMOND NECKLACE

Vocabulary: Synonyms are words with similar meanings. Antonyms are words with opposite meanings. Underline the synonym and circle the antonym of the boldfaced word in each word group. Then use the numbered words to fill in the blanks in the sentences below.

1. **blaming**	criticizing	trying	praising	solving
2. **facts**	puns	lies	wishes	truth
3. **racket**	proof	uproar	silence	gamble
4. **guarding**	ignoring	following	leading	watching

· ·

1. Our watchdog always made a _____ when the mail carrier came to our door.

2. The jury made its decision after hearing all the _____.

3. My brother is always _____ me for things I did not do.

4. We wondered who was _____ the bank while the building was under repair.

Clues:

As you read "The Case of the Diamond Necklace," write down any clues in the story that might help you solve the case.

```



```

The Case of the Diamond Necklace (cont.)

Questions:

1. What did Mrs. Van Tweedle plan to do with the necklace?
2. Why was Chief Brown at the party?
3. Why was Miss Stark wearing the necklace?
4. Why did Miss Stark go to the guest room upstairs?
5. What sounds did Chief Brown hear from Miss Stark's room?
6. What did Chief Brown think happened to the necklace?
7. Why did Encyclopedia Brown want the guest room searched?

Questions for Discussion:

1. Do you agree with Encyclopedia that "every crook makes one mistake"? Or, is there such a thing as a "perfect crime"?
2. If you were Chief Brown, would you have handled the case differently once you heard the scream and shots from the guest room?

Science Connection:

Diamonds are made from carbon—the same material as coal. Do some research to find out how diamonds become clear crystals that are hard and beautiful. Also, find out where and how diamonds are mined and how they are cut into beautiful jewels.

Writing Activity:

Pretend you are Miss Stark, the would-be diamond thief. Write a confession that tells how you tried to steal your friend's necklace. Provide a step-by-step account of what you did at the party and how you hoped to get away with the crime.

THE CASE OF THE KNIFE IN THE WATERMELON

Vocabulary: Use the words in the Word Box and the clues below to complete the crossword puzzle.

```
                        WORD BOX
    attempt    expenses    fingerprints    muttered    plunge
```

Across

2. spoke with your lips half-closed so people wouldn't hear your angry words

4. these provide clues that someone was on the scene

5. make an effort

Down

1. quick way to get into a pool or into trouble

3. list these on your budget

Clues:

As you read "The Case of the Knife in the Watermelon," write down any clues in the story that might help you solve the case.

The Case of the Knife in the Watermelon (cont.)

Questions:

1. Why was there a knife in one of Mr. Patch's watermelons?
2. Why did Encyclopedia suspect the knife belonged to one of the Lions?
3. Why couldn't Encyclopedia find fingerprints on the knife?
4. Why did the members of the Lions start quarreling with each other?
5. Why didn't Encyclopedia believe what Corky said about his knife?

Questions for Discussion:

1. Do you think it was all right for Encyclopedia to trick the Lions by telling them that the police would take fingerprints? After all, he knew there were no prints on the knife.
2. Can Encyclopedia be sure that the knife belongs to Corky just because that boy lied and acted in a suspicious manner?

Science Connection:

Fingerprints help detectives catch criminals. Do some research to find out about fingerprinting. Learn how detectives dust for fingerprints and explain how fingerprints are classified and used for identification. You may want to take your own fingerprints and compare them to those of your classmates.

Writing Activity:

Write a different ending for "The Case of the Knife in the Watermelon." Instead of a jacket with the letter "L" on it, make up a new clue that leads Encyclopedia to a different suspect. Then tell how Encyclopedia gets this person to admit to owning the knife or breaking into Mr. Patch's store.

THE CASE OF THE MISSING ROLLER SKATES

Vocabulary: Draw a line from each word on the left to its definition on the right. Then use the numbered words to fill in the blanks in the sentences below.

1. exclaimed
2. certainty
3. calm
4. suspect
5. lead

    a. peaceful; tranquil
    b. said suddenly with strong feeling
    c. person thought to be guilty
    d. information that shows the way
    e. state of being sure

. . . .

1. The police observed the _____ for several days before making an arrest.

2. A caller on the hotline gave us an important _____ to help us solve the crime.

3. All the fans _____ how happy they were when the home team won the championship.

4. It is necessary to remain _____ in an emergency.

5. I could not reply with _____ that I had seen the robber leave the bank because it had been foggy that day.

Clues:

As you read "The Case of the Missing Roller Skates," write down any clues in the story that might help you solve the case.

The Case of the Missing Roller Skates (cont.)

Questions:

1. Where was Encyclopedia when his skates were stolen? Where were the skates?

2. What conclusion did Encyclopedia draw about the thiefs identity?

3. How did Encyclopedia get Billy Haggerty's name as a lead in the case?

4. What did Billy say to Encyclopedia that gave him away?

Questions for Discussion:

1. Have you ever had anything stolen from you? Did you try to get it back? How?

2. Can you think of any real-life situations in which a wrong-doer did or said something that gave him or her away? Describe the situation.

Writing Activity:

Write a journal entry that Encyclopedia might have written after getting the stolen roller skates back. Tell how he probably felt about this case and about his detective work in general.

THE CASE OF THE CHAMPION EGG SPINNER

Vocabulary: Some words in English have more than one meaning. Read each word and its definitions. Then figure out which definition fits the way the word is used in the sentence that follows. Write the letter of the definition you choose on the line at the right.

match

    a. contest

    b. someone or something that is like another

1. The better player will win the <u>match</u>.   _____

counter

    a. person who adds up numbers

    b. long, narrow table with stools

2. When I am in a hurry, I sit at the <u>counter</u> instead of a table in the restaurant.   _____

beat

    a. win over in a race

    b. stir vigorously

3. The fastest runner <u>beat</u> everyone else.   _____

Clues:

As you read "The Case of the Champion Egg Spinner," write down any clues in the story that might help you solve the case.

Questions:

1. Where did Encyclopedia first see Eddie, the champion, spinning an egg? What happened to Eddie's egg?
2. Why were Encyclopedia's friends worried about the egg spinning contest?
3. At the spinning contest, what did Charlie signal to Encyclopedia when he raised one finger?
4. What did Encyclopedia ask Eddie and Charlie to do just before the contest began?
5. What did Eddie do to the egg that Charlie marked for him?

The Case of the Champion Egg Spinner (cont.)

Questions for Discussion:

1. How did Encyclopedia use his sharp powers of observation to crack this case?

2. Have you ever been in a game or contest where someone cheated? What is the best way to deal with this kind of situation?

Humor:

A pun is a play on words. Usually puns are funny because a word has at least two meanings in the same sentence. Read these "egg" puns that the author included in "The Case of the Champion Egg Spinner." Which word in each sentence has a double meaning? Tell why you think each is funny?

*   "Eddie Phelan's egg beat everything," said Charlie.
    "Who is this Eddie Phelan?" asked Encyclopedia. "A human egg beater."

*   "This case smells rotten," said Encyclopedia.

*   "The case of the champion egg spinner is cracked," Encyclopedia said mysteriously.

Math/Science Connection

Try spinning your own eggs. Work with a raw egg and time how long it spins. Then hardboil the same egg and spin and time it again. Calculate how much longer on average the hardboiled egg spins.

Make a suggestion, or hypothesis, that explains why the hardboiled egg spins longer. If a small scale is available, see whether the weight of the egg changes after hardboiling. If not, what other explanations can you suggest?

Writing Activity:

Unlike Idaville, where Encyclopedia has solved every crime and mystery, your town probably has a few cases that still need solutions. Think of one that you have heard or read about. Write down the facts of the case. Then pretend you hired Encyclopedia to solve it. Write what he might do to solve it cleverly. Once you have your mystery and solution, write it in the form of an Encyclopedia Brown case.

CLOZE ACTIVITY

The following passage is taken from "The Case of Natty Nat." Read it through completely. Then fill in each blank with a word that makes sense. Afterwards, you may compare your words with those of the author.

Idaville, however, only *looked* like the usual American town. It was, really,

most _____.[1]

For nearly a whole year no criminal _____[2] escaped arrest and no

boy or girl _____[3] got away with breaking a single law _____[4]

Idaville.

This was partly because the town's policemen _____[5] clever and

brave. But mostly it was _____[6] Chief Brown was Encyclopedia's father. His

hardest cases _____[7] solved by Encyclopedia during dinner in the

_____[8] red brick house on Rover Avenue.

Everyone _____[9] the state thought that Idaville had about

_____[10] smartest policemen in the world.

Of course, _____[11] knew a boy was the mastermind behind the

town's _____[12] force.

You wouldn't guess it by looking _____[13] Encyclopedia. He looked

like almost any fifth-grade _____[14] and acted line one, too—except that

_____[15] never talked about himself.

Mr. Brown never _____[16] a word about the advice his son

_____[17] him. Who would believe that his best detective was only ten years

old?

POST-READING ACTIVITIES AND DISCUSSION QUESTIONS

1. With a partner or small group of classmates role-playa scene from one of Encyclopedia's cases. You might want to choose one of these scenes or you might choose a scene of your own:

   - Encyclopedia looking at Bugs Meany's sword in "The Case of the Civil War Sword."
   - Encyclopedia talking to Bill Haggerty in "The Case of the Missing Roller Skates."
   - Encyclopedia challenging Eddie Phelan in "The Case of the Champion Egg Spinner."

2. Encyclopedia solved ten cases in this book. Which case did you like best? Which did you like least? Make a list called Encyclopedia's Top Ten cases. List the cases in the book in the order in which you liked them, beginning with your favorite case. Then see if your friends' lists are similar.

3. Suppose you were going to make a movie about Encyclopedia Brown. Whom would you choose among your classmates to play the roles of Encyclopedia, Sally Kimball, and Bugs Meany? Which cases would you include, and which would you leave out?

4. Have you read any other mysteries in which young people solve cases? Give a short talk to your classmates about a favorite mystery. Tell how this mystery is different from *Encyclopedia Brown, Boy Detective*.

5. Read another book in the *Encyclopedia Brown* series by Donald Sobol. Write a review that tells how it is similar and different from *Encyclopedia Brown, Boy Detective*.

6. Pick a favorite scene from one of Encyclopedia's cases. Draw an illustration or make a diorama of the scene that would help readers see the action that is taking place.

SUGGESTIONS FOR FURTHER READING

Anderson, Mary. *The Mystery of the Missing Painting*. Scholastic.

*   Atwater, Richard, and Florence Atwater. *Mr. Popper's Penguins*. Little, Brown.

*   Bellairs, John. *House With a Clock in its Walls*. Penguin.

Bulla, Robert Clyde. *The Ghost of Windy Hill*. Crowell.

*   Cleary, Beverly. *The Mouse and the Motorcycle*. HarperCollins.

*   Fitzgerald, John D. *The Great Brain*. Random House.

         _____. *The Great Brain at the Academy*. Random House.

*   Howe, James, and Deborah Howe. *Bunnicula*. Simon & Schuster.

Kehret, Pet. *Deadly Stranger*. Troll.

Levy, Elizabeth. *The Computer That Said Steal Me*. Scholastic.

*   Naylor, Phyllis. *Shiloh*. Simon & Schuster.

*   Peterson, John. *The Littles*. Scholastic.

Roberts, Willo Davis. *The Girl with the Silver Eyes*. Scholastic.

Saunders, Susan. *Mystery Cat*. Random House.

*   Warner, Gertrude. *The Boxcar Children*. Albert Whitman.

Wright, Betty Ren. *The Dollhouse Murders*. Scholastic.

Some Other Books by Donald Sobol

Encyclopedia Brown and the Case of the Secret Pitch. Random House.

Encyclopedia Brown Finds the Clues. Random House.

Encyclopedia Brown Gets His Man. Random House.

Encyclopedia Brown Solves Them All. Random House.

Encyclopedia Brown Keeps the Peace. Random House.

Encyclopedia Brown Saves the Day. Random House.

*   NOVEL-TIES Study Guides are available for these titles.

ANSWER KEY

The Case of Natty Nat

Vocabulary: 1. d 2. c 3. e 4. a 5. b; 1. dingy 2. natty 3. observation 4. criminal 5. mastermind

Questions: 1. Mr. Brown, the police chief, discussed any unsolved cases with his son Encyclopedia Brown, who always managed to suggest a solution. 2. Chief Brown thought that Natty Nat was the robber because Mr. Dillon, the owner of the store, claimed he was and described him based on newspaper accounts. 3. It became clear that Mr. Dillon was lying when he mentioned seeing the belt on the back of Nat's coat, something he could not have seen.

The Case of the Scattered Cards

Vocabulary: 1. b 2. c 3. d 4. a; 1. blackmail 2. murder 3. kidnapping 4. robbery

Questions: 1. Clarence claimed he found the tent and put it up two days earlier only to have Bugs Meany take it over and force him to go away. 2. Bugs Meany and the Tigers claimed that they found the tent and had put it up that same day. 3. Since it had been raining for two days, Encyclopedia knew the ground inside the tent should have been wet if Bugs had really put up the tent that day. 4. The cards that Encyclopedia scattered on the ground were dry, showing that Bugs couldn't put up the tent that day.

The Case of the Civil War Sword

Vocabulary: 1. gasped 2. corrected 3. presented 4. sneered 5. grinning; 1. presented 2. corrected 3. grinning 4. sneered 5. gasped

Questions: 1. Peter wanted Encyclopedia to find out whether a sword that Bugs hoped to trade was once really owned by General Stonewall Jackson. 2. When Peter told Encyclopedia about the trade, he suggested to Peter that any trade with Bugs would be suspect. When Bugs saw Encyclopedia, he called him "Mr. Brains" and "Mr. Know-it-all." 3. The message on the blade said the sword had been given to General Jackson by his men a month after the First Battle of Bull Run in 1861. 4. Encyclopedia warned against the trade since the Southerners would not have known in 1861 that there would be a second Battle of Bull Run the following year and so would not have placed the word "First" on the sword blade.

The Case of Merko's Grandson

Vocabulary: 1. challenged 2. champions 3. snarled 4. triumph 5. referee 6. inheritance; *Message* — listen

Questions: 1. Bugs and the Tigers rallied around Encyclopedia because they disliked Sally more than Encyclopedia. Sally was a girl who could best Bugs and his friends at softball; she also beat up Bugs for bullying a younger child. 2. Sally wasn't content to prove that she was the best athlete in the class; she wanted to prove that she was the smartest. Therefore, she had to challenge Encyclopedia. 3. The kids had a mystery-telling contest; Sally told the mystery, complete with clues, and Encyclopedia had to solve it. 4. The great Merko was a famous trapeze artist; Merko's will said that her money should go to a grandson in forty years. If there was no grandson, the money would go to the nearest relative. 5. The kids assumed that Merko was a man. Sally said that Merko was not Fred Gibson's grandfather. Encyclopedia surprised everyone by realizing that Merko was Gibson's grandmother.

The Case of the Bank Robber

Vocabulary: 1. b 2. d 3. c 4. a 5. e; 1. beggar 2. resisted 3. recognize 4. features 5. distinguishing

Questions: 1. Encyclopedia and Sally saw a bank robbery. 2. The robber ran into a blind beggar and for a moment seemed to be wrangling with him. 3. When the police caught the robber, he didn't have the stolen money; moreover, no one at the bank could make a positive identification of him. 4. Encyclopedia wanted to talk to Blind Tom to see if he was aware of anything unusual about the robber. 5. Encyclopedia decided not to talk to Blind Tom because he deduced that Tom was not blind. Tom, as an accomplice in the crime, received the money from the robber as they pretended to wrangle in the street.

The Case of the Happy Nephew

Vocabulary: 1. proof 2. arrest 3. alibi 4. eyewitness; 1. eyewitness 2. arrest 3. alibi 4. proof

Questions: 1. The crime was the robbery of a bake shop. 2. The eyewitness claimed to have seen John Abbot running from the shop at the time of the robbery. 3. Abbot said that he had been on the road all day, just reaching home after a 600-mile car trip. 4. Encyclopedia noticed that Abbot's car hood was not hot, making it improbable that he had just finished a long car trip.

The Case of the Diamond Necklace

Vocabulary: 1. blaming; S – criticizing, A – praising 2. facts: S – truth, A – lies 3. racket: S – uproar, A – silence 4. guarding: S – watching, A – ignoring; 1. racket 2. facts 3. blaming 4. guarding

Questions: 1. Mrs. Van Tweedle planned to auction off the necklace for charity. 2. Chief Brown was at the party to guard the necklace. 3. Miss Stark was wearing the necklace so that people could notice it. 4. Miss Stark went to the guest room because she claimed she didn't feel well and needed to lie down. 5. Outside the room, Chief Brown heard a scream and then two shots. Chief Brown thought the necklace had been stolen by a thief who escaped through a window. 7. Encyclopedia wanted the guest room searched because Miss Stark claimed not to have seen anything, yet she screamed before the two shots. Encyclopedia thought she had hidden the necklace in the room and only pretended it was stolen.

The Case of the Knife in the Watermelon

Vocabulary: Across — 2. muttered 4. fingerprints 5. attempt; Down — 1. plunge 3. expenses

Questions: 1. A boy who broke into Mr. Patch's store plunged his knife into the melon by mistake as he was trying to get away. 2. Mr. Patch said the would-be robber was wearing a jacket with a big "L" on the back. 3. Mr. Patch accidentally wiped off the prints when he was cleaning up some spilled flour. 4. The Lions were afraid that one of them would be blamed for the crime; each tried to clear himself by implicating another. 5. Corky said his knife had a longer blade than the one in the watermelon; Encyclopedia pointed out that he couldn't have known the length of the blade since it was plunged inside the melon.

The Case of the Missing Roller Skates

Vocabulary: 1. b 2. e 3. a 4. c 5. d; 1. suspect 2. lead 3. exclaimed 4. calm 5. certainty
Questions: 1. When the skates were stolen, Encyclopedia was at Dr. Wilson's office, having a tooth removed; his skates were outside in the waiting room. 2. Encyclopedia decided that the thief was a boy or a girl, not a grown-up. 3. Encyclopedia questioned all the receptionists in the medical arts building to see if any kids had been in when he was there: the only young patient was Billy Haggerty. 4. Billy Haggerty said that he didn't know anything about Dr. Vivian Wilson, Encyclopedia's doctor. Then he gave himself away by revealing that he knew Dr. Wilson was a dentist, and, despite the name Vivian, was a man.

The Case of the Champion Egg Spinner

Vocabulary: 1. a 2. b 3. a
Questions: 1. Encyclopedia saw Eddie, whom he did not know, spin an egg on the counter of Mr. O'Hara's luncheonette. Eddie's egg spun off the counter and broke on the floor. Mr. O'Hara swept it up. 2. The friends were worried since Eddie was a much better spinner and always won the items they bet. 3. Charlie signaled that the egg Eddie was spinning was indeed the one Charlie marked for him to use. 4. Encyclopedia asked Eddie and Charlie to switch eggs. 5. Eddie hardboiled the egg that Charlie marked, making it easier to spin.